Ruth
Hawes

Lesson
ALL-IN-TWO

L E

PIANO

Adventures® *by Nancy and Randall Faber*

THE BASIC PIANO METHOD

Student's Name: _____

Production: Jon Ophoff
Cover and Illustrations: Terpstra Design, San Francisco
Engraving: Dovetree Productions, Inc.

Book Only ISBN 978-1-61677-686-2
Book & CD ISBN 978-1-61677-687-9

Progress Chart

C, G, and F Scales Hands Together

- Play these scales hands separately, then **slowly play hands together.**

- "Shape" your scales with a *crescendo* going up and a *diminuendo* going down.

C Major Scale   *Finger 3s play together.*

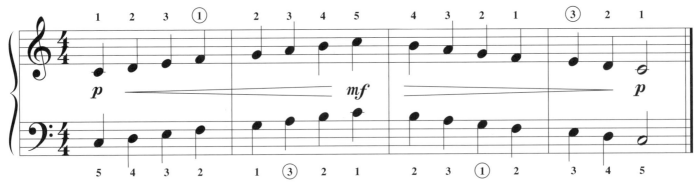

G Major Scale   *Finger 3s play together.*

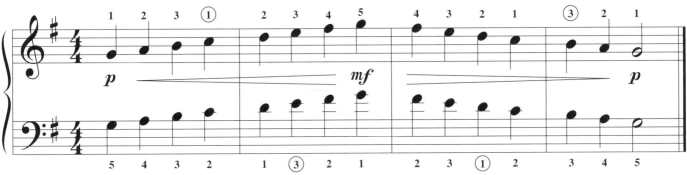

F Major Scale   *Thumbs play together on C.*

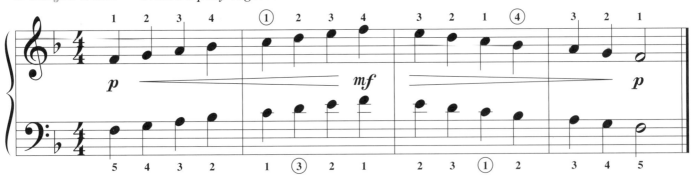

C, G, and F Scale Challenges

For your next lessons, try these additional scale challenges!

1. Play each scale hands together **with eyes closed.**

2. Play the scale 5 times **hands together.**
   Begin playing in the LOWEST octaves.
   Move your hands 1 octave HIGHER for each repeat.

THE ULTIMATE SCALE WARM-UPS

Transposing Challenge

- Play as written, then transpose to **G** and **F major**. Notice the L.H. thumb starts on the *tonic*, then steps down to the *leading note* in bar 2.

Little March

Key of _____ Major

Daniel Gottlob Türk
(1750-1813, Germany)
original form

Allegro (♩ = 132-152)

f

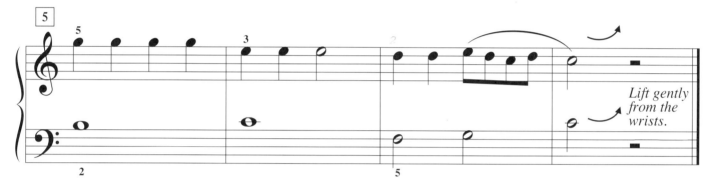

Lift gently from the wrists.

I, IV, and V7 Chord Review

I, **IV**, and **V7** chords are the **primary** (most important) chords in any key.

- Review these I, IV, and V7 chords in G major. Then transpose to **C** and **F major**.

Blocked chords

mf

Say: I   IV   I   V7   I   I   IV   V7   I

- Review these I, IV, and V7 chords in F major. Then transpose to **G** and **C major**.

Waltz pattern

mp

Say: I   IV   I   V7   I

Tech & Perf page 4 (Sighing), page 7 (Scale Round-Offs)

The Alberti Bass

The *Alberti bass* is a common L.H. broken chord pattern named after the Italian composer Domenico Alberti.

• Notice the pattern: bottom-top-middle-top.

Warm-up

I chord

IV chord

V7 chord

• Play the I chord Alberti bass example to end.

Musical Form: Ternary or ABA

Ternary form or **ABA** form means three sections—
an **A** section, **B** section, and a return to the **A** section.
If the A section is slightly changed, we label it **A¹**.

• Write **A**, **B**, or **A¹** in the boxes given.

Looking-Glass River

Key of _____ Major

Andante (♩ = 112-120)

(light thumb)

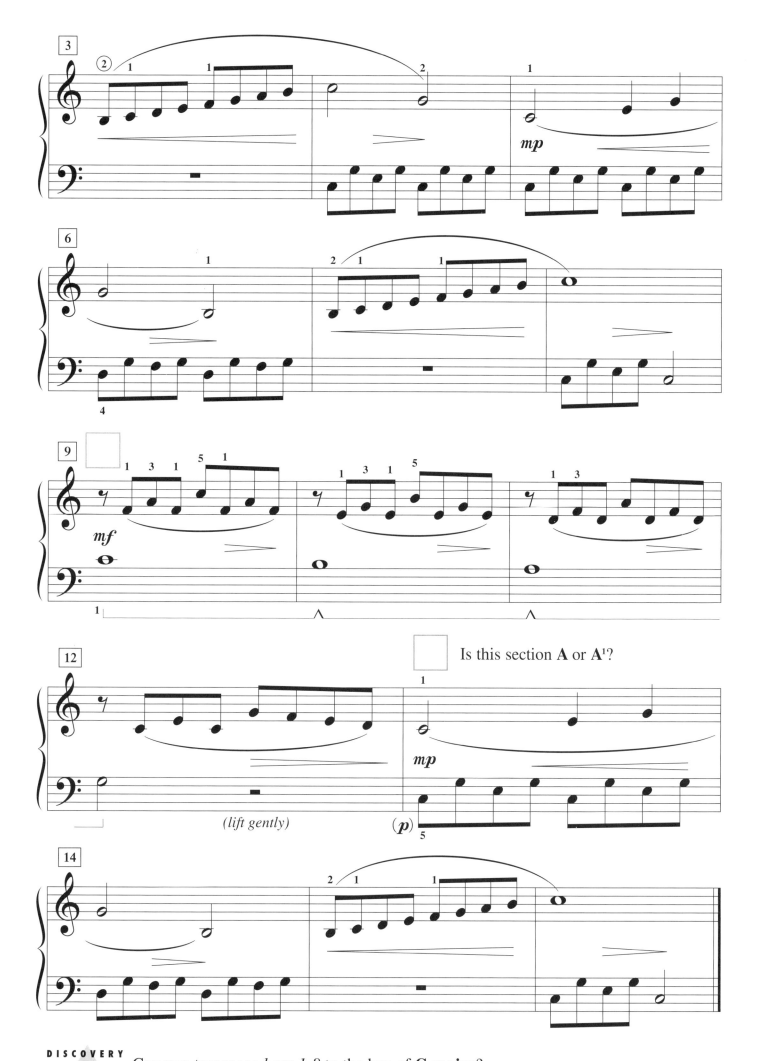

Is this section **A** or **A¹**?

(lift gently)

DISCOVERY

Can you transpose *bars 1-8* to the key of **G major**?
Congratulations on transposing outside a 5-finger pattern!

7

Syncopation occurs when notes BETWEEN the beats are stressed.

- Tap and count aloud with your teacher. Notice the syncopation in the second bar.

- Now play three times on a **I** chord, a **IV** chord, and a **V7** chord in the key of **G major**.

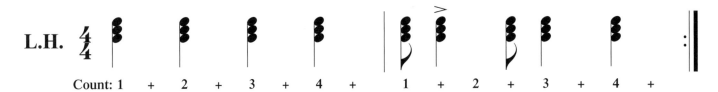

L.H.

Count: 1 + 2 + 3 + 4 + 1 + 2 + 3 + 4 +

Review: Accidentals

Flats or sharps in the music but *not* in the key signature are called **accidentals**. The natural (♮) is also an accidental.

- Point out an accidental.

Yellow Bird

Key of _____ Major

West Indies Folk Song
arranged

Cheerfully (♩ = 104)

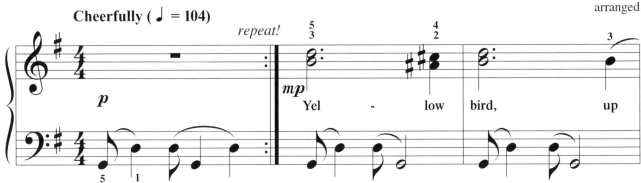

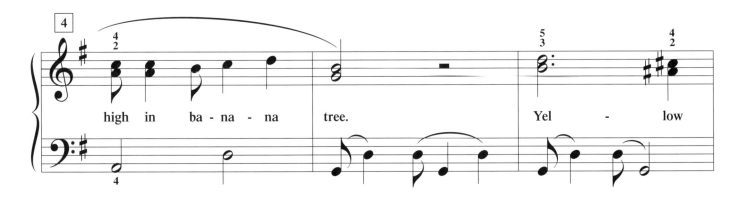

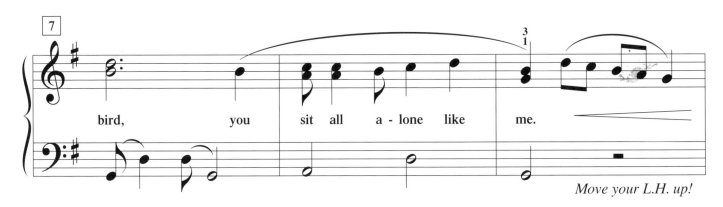

Move your L.H. up!

🕊 Tech & Perf page 5 (Finger Springs), page 9 (Procession in G)

DISCOVERY

Harmony Check: Write I, IV, or V7 in the boxes for *bars 10-17*.
Can you transpose this piece up to **C Major**? Your teacher will help you.

Edvard Grieg wrote the music for the theatre play *Peer Gynt* by Henrik Ibsen.
This colourful folk-tale relates the adventures of Peer Gynt, a Norwegian mountain boy,
as he journeys to the four corners of the world.

Morning was written for Act IV of the play,
with Peer Gynt having arrived in Africa.

Morning

Key of _____ Major

Edvard Grieg
(1843-1907, Norway)
arranged

- First play hands separately, noticing the
  fingering and chord changes.

Moderately (♩ = 100-120)

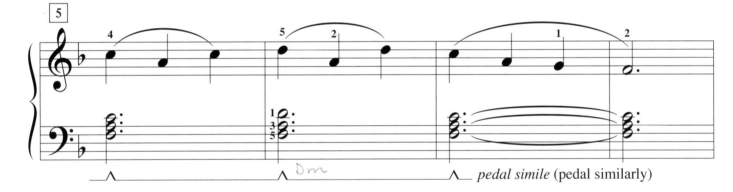

pedal simile (pedal similarly)

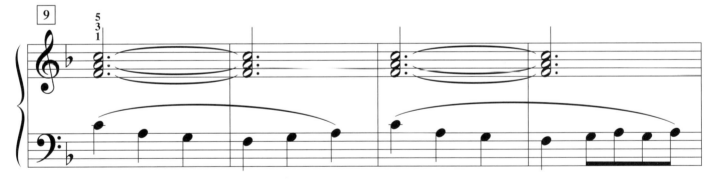

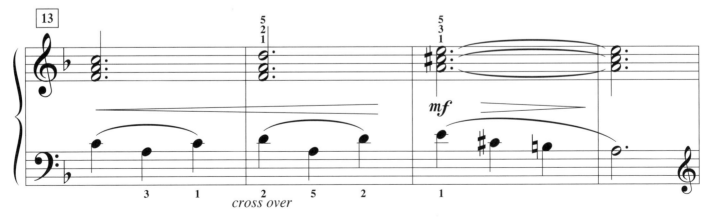

DISCOVERY

Where does the theme first appear in **A major**? *bar* ____
Where does the theme return to **F major**? *bar* ____

Swing Rhythm (common in jazz and blues)

In **swing rhythm**, quavers (eighth notes) are played in a *long-short* pattern.*

- Your teacher will tap and chant these quavers in swing rhythm.
  Now try it together!

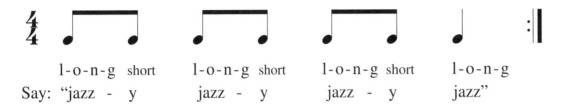

l-o-n-g short   l-o-n-g short   l-o-n-g short   l-o-n-g

Say: "jazz - y   jazz - y   jazz - y   jazz"

*Teacher Note:

Swing Rhythm Warm-up

- First play the L.H. separately with **even quavers**.
  The circles will alert you to fingering changes.

- Next play hands together with the quavers in a
  long-short **swing rhythm**.

If the **tempo mark** includes the word "swing,"
play the quavers with a *long-short* swing rhythm.

Cool Walkin' Bass

Moderate swing (♩ = 108-116)

Teacher Duet: (Student plays *as written*)

Write C, G, and F Major Scales

The major scale has 7 notes called **scale degrees**.
A scale is created from tones and semitones.

Review: The semitones are between *scale degrees 3–4* and *degrees 7–8*.
All the other intervals are tones.

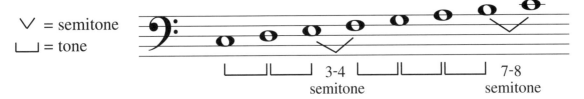

1. • Write each scale below. Number the scale degrees 1-8.
   • Use a ⎍ to mark the *tones*. Use a ∨ to mark the *semitones*.

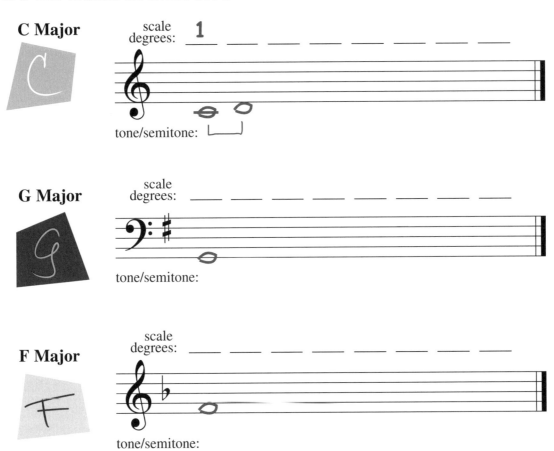

C Major

scale degrees: **1** ___ ___ ___ ___ ___ ___ ___

tone/semitone:

G Major

scale degrees: ___ ___ ___ ___ ___ ___ ___ ___

tone/semitone:

F Major

scale degrees: ___ ___ ___ ___ ___ ___ ___ ___

tone/semitone:

2. Name each key signature. Then circle **I**, **IV**, or **V7** for the chord given.

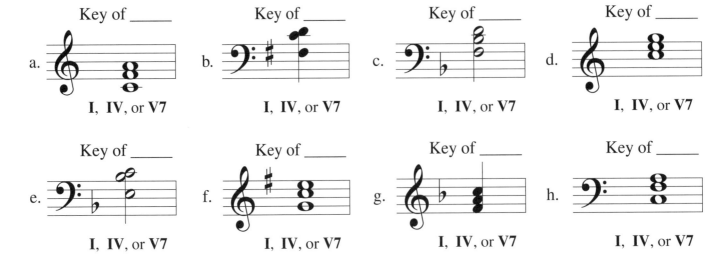

Key of _____   Key of _____   Key of _____   Key of _____

a.   b.   c.   d.

I, IV, or V7   I, IV, or V7   I, IV, or V7   I, IV, or V7

Key of _____   Key of _____   Key of _____   Key of _____

e.   f.   g.   h.

I, IV, or V7   I, IV, or V7   I, IV, or V7   I, IV, or V7

14

Harmonise with I, IV, and V7 Chords

3. We can **harmonise** a melody with **I** , **IV**, and **V7 chords**. Play and *listen* to each example.

Use the **I** chord for
scale degrees 1-3-5.

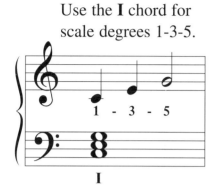

Use the **IV** chord for
scale degrees 1-4-6.

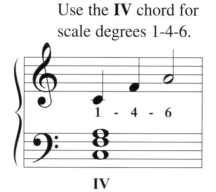

Use the **V7** chord for
scale degrees 2-4-5.

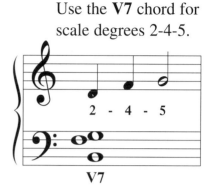

4.
- Notice the key signature, then play each melody.
- Now harmonise by writing **I**, **IV**, or **V7** in the boxes.
- Play each with solid chords.

You Harmonise!

5.  Close your eyes and *listen*. Your teacher will play example **a** or **b**.
Open your eyes and circle the chord pattern you heard.

Teacher Note: Play in the keys of C, G, or F. Play solid chords or an Alberti bass!

1a.   **I V7 I V7**
or
b.   **I V7 V7 I**

2a.   **I IV I V7**
or
b.   **I I I IV**

3a.   **I IV IV I**
or
b.   **I IV V7 I**

15

Interval of a Seventh (7th)

Review: An interval is the distance between 2 notes on the keyboard or stave.

New: The interval of a **7th** covers 7 keys and 7 letter names.

- Play the interval below (D up to C). Listen to the sound.

A 7th is one key smaller than an octave.

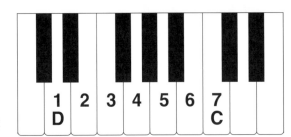

Ex:

1. Find 7ths

Play these 7ths on the keyboard.

- L.H. finger 5 on E. **Play up a 7th.**
  Did you land on D?

- L.H. finger 5 on A. **Play up a 7th.**
  Did you land on G?

- R.H. finger 5 on F. **Play down a 7th.**
  Did you land on G?

- R.H. finger 5 on B. **Play down a 7th.**
  Did you land on C?

2. Read 7ths

What does the interval of a 7th have in common with the interval of a 3rd and a 5th?
It is always *line-to-line* or *space-to-space*.

- Play R.H. and *listen!*

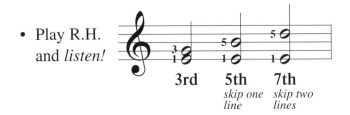

3rd | 5th | 7th
skip one line | *skip two lines*

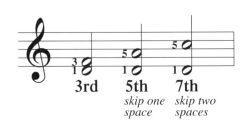

3rd | 5th | 7th
skip one space | *skip two spaces*

3. Listen for 7ths

- Close your eyes. Listen as your teacher plays the interval of a **3rd**, **5th**, or **7th**.

- Name the interval you hear.

A 3rd sounds sweet. A 5th sounds hollow. A 7th sounds more dissonant.

Teacher Note: Play the notes of each interval separately, then together.

- Play and *listen* to the intervals grow from a 2nd to an octave.

- Then transpose to **G major**. Remember the F♯. Transpose to **F major**. Remember the B♭.

Interval Warm-ups

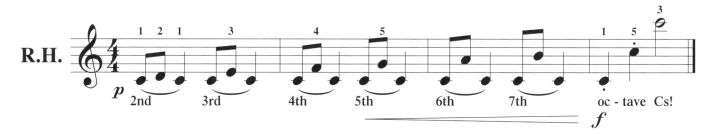

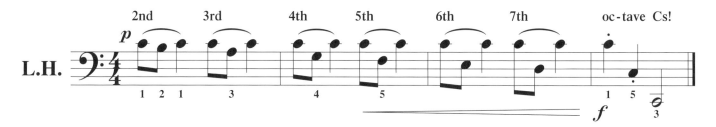

𝐂 **= Common Time**

𝐂 is the symbol for common time.
Common time is the same as $\frac{4}{4}$.

- Circle the 𝐂 in the music.

7th St. Blues

Key of _____ Major

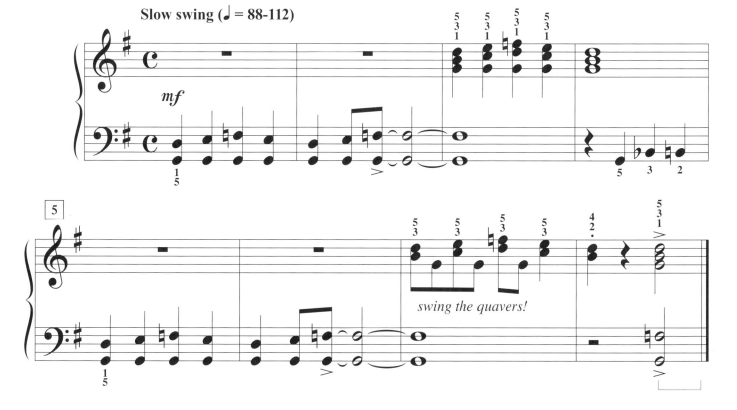

tenuto or **stress mark** ♩

This mark means to hold the note its full value.
Hint: Press deeply into the key.

Lunar Eclipse

- Name the opening R.H. broken chord.
  Is it major or minor? _____

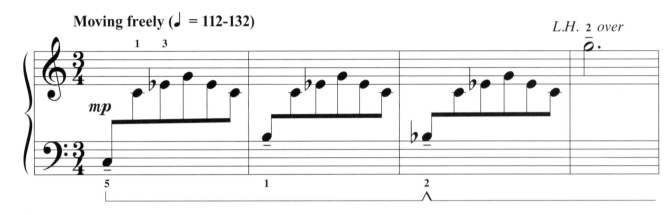

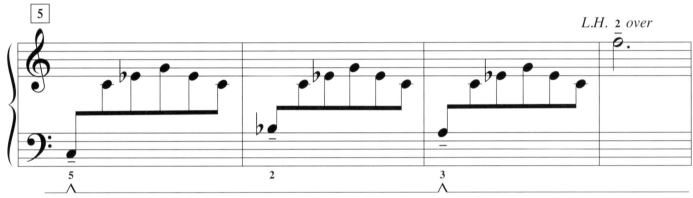

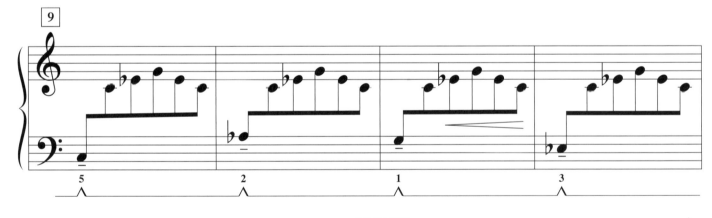

Tech & Perf page 13 (The Back-up Singers)

Note: In *bars 17-20*, the R.H. plays both the melody and harmony (two voices). Play the upper voice *mf* with a rich tone. Play the thumb *lightly* on the inner voice.

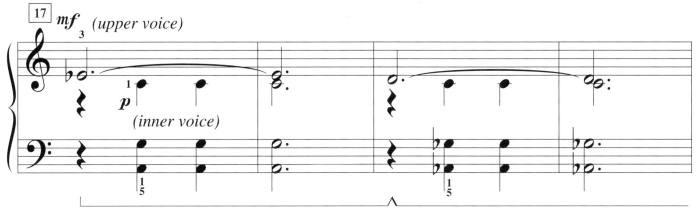

D.C. al Coda – means "from the top to the Coda."
Return to the beginning and play to the Coda sign ϕ, then jump to the *Coda* (ending).

Common Time to Cut Time

$\mathbf{C}$ = $\dfrac{4}{4}$ beats in a bar

the ♩ gets one beat

Let's cut it in half!

$\mathbf{¢}$ = $\dfrac{2}{2}$ beats in a bar

the ♩ gets one beat

Cut time is also known as *alla breve*.

- Tap quickly, feeling **2 beats** per bar. Remember, the ♩ gets the beat.

- First, play slowly in common time. Feel **4 beats** per bar.

- When ready, play faster in cut time. Feel **2 beats** per bar.

Cossack Ride

Allegro (♩ = 112)

Musical Form Check: Circle the correct form. (Notice the A section repeats.)

A A B A   A A B Coda   A A B A Coda

ostinato – a musical pattern that is repeated over and over.

This piece uses a L.H. 7th as an ostinato.

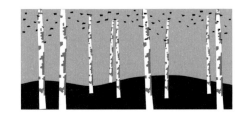

Land of the Silver Birch

Canadian Folk Melody
Words by Pauline Johnson
arranged

Flowing gently, "in two" (♩ = 69-80)

1. Land of the sil - ver birch, home of the bea - ver,
2. High on a rock - y ledge, I'll build my wig - wam

Where still the might - y moose wan - ders at will.
Close by the wat - er's edge, si - lent and still.

Blue lake and rock - y shores, I will re - turn once more.

cross over ②

Repeat softly with R.H. 8ᵛᵃ higher.

Boom de de boom, boom, Boom de de boom, boom, Boom de de boom, boom, boom.
last time rit.

Compose a short piece of your own using the L.H. ostinato above.
Use the D minor 5-finger scale for your R.H. melody.

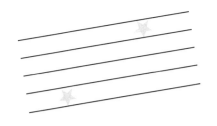

Identify and Write 7ths

1. Identify each interval as a **3rd**, **5th**, or **7th**. Count each line and space, including the *first* and *last* note.

Ex. __5th__

b. _____

c. _____

d. _____

e. _____

f. _____

g. _____

h. _____

i. _____

j. _____

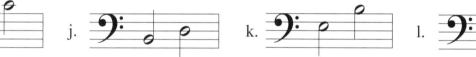
k. _____

l. _____

2. Write a **7th** up or down from each note. Then name both notes.

a.
note names: _____ _____
up a 7th

b. _____ _____
down a 7th

c. _____ _____
up a 7th

d. _____ _____
down a 7th

e. _____ _____
up a 7th

f. _____ _____
up a 7th

The Triplet

Sometimes **3** quavers equal a crotchet. This is called a **triplet.**

The italic 3 above indicates a triplet, not finger number 3.

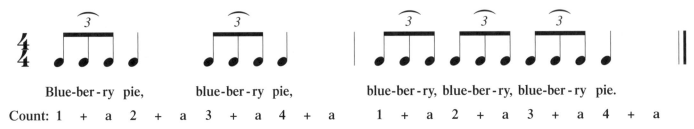

Count: 1   +   a   1   +   a

• Tap and count aloud with your teacher.

Blue-ber-ry pie,   blue-ber-ry pie,   blue-ber-ry, blue-ber-ry, blue-ber-ry pie.

Count: 1 + a 2 + a 3 + a 4 + a   1 + a 2 + a 3 + a 4 + a

• First play the R.H. separately for *bars 1-8*, counting aloud.

• Play the L.H. separately for *bars 5-8*. Where does this pattern recur?

Sonatina in C

William Duncombe
(18th century, England)
original form

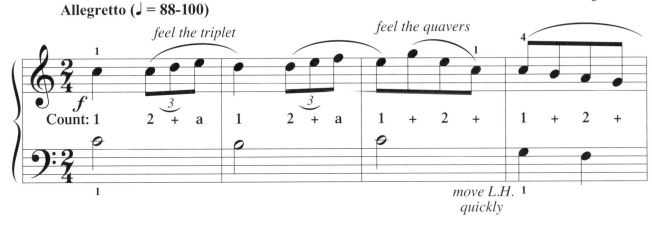

Allegretto (♩ = 88-100)

feel the triplet   *feel the quavers*

Count: 1   2 + a   1   2 + a   1 + 2 +   1 + 2 +

move L.H. quickly

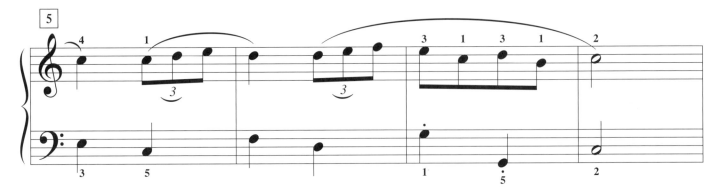

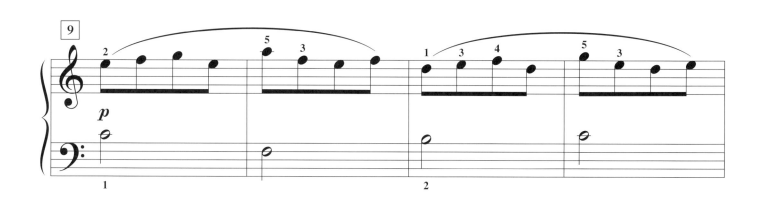

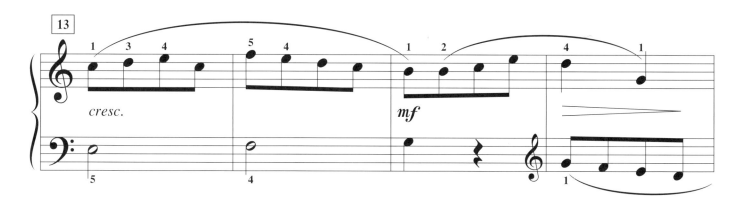

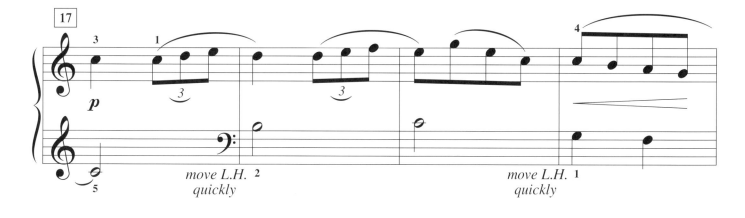

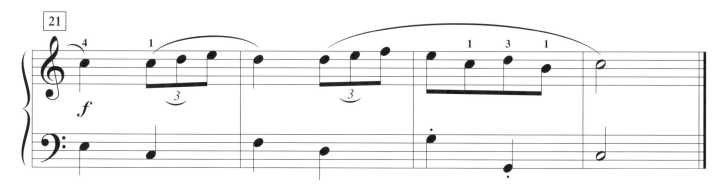

Musical Form Check: Label the sections of this piece.

Name the form: _____

New Dynamic Sign

$\boldsymbol{\mathit{ff}}$ – *fortissimo*

Fortissimo means very loud, louder than *forte*.

Malagueña*

Pablo de Sarasate
(1844-1908, Spain)
arranged

• Is your L.H. playing softer on beats 2 and 3?

*A *malagueña* is a Spanish dance from the town of Malaga.

Tech & Perf pages 18-19 (Bittersweet Blues)

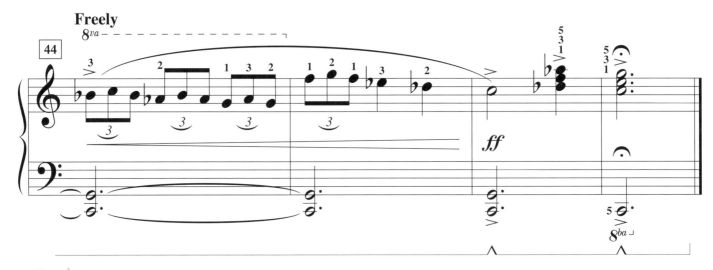

DISCOVERY

In this piece, find and circle a **triplet** on beat 1, beat 2, and beat 3.

Draw the Bar Lines!

1. Add bar lines after every **2 beats**. Then write "1-2" under the correct notes.

2. Add bar lines after every **3 beats**. Then write "1-2-3" under the correct notes.

3. Add bar lines after every **4 beats**. Then write "1-2-3-4" under the correct notes.

4. Tap each rhythm above for your teacher with the metronome ticking at ♩ = 84.

5. Put an X through each *incorrect* bar. It may have too many or too few beats.

6. Choose a time signature: **2/4**, **3/4**, or **4/4** and write your own rhythm using triplets.

↑
time
signature

7. Your teacher will tap a short rhythm that uses the triplet. Listen and tap it back.

Teacher Note: Create your own rhythm patterns. Two examples are given below.

Key of A Minor

Every major key has a minor key that shares the *same* key signature.
This minor key is called the RELATIVE MINOR.

The relative minor starts on the **6th degree of the major scale**.
You can also count **3 semitones down** from the tonic of the major key.

The key of A minor is the relative minor of C major.

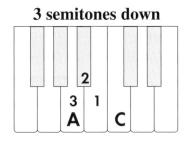

1. Play each scale and *listen* to the scound.

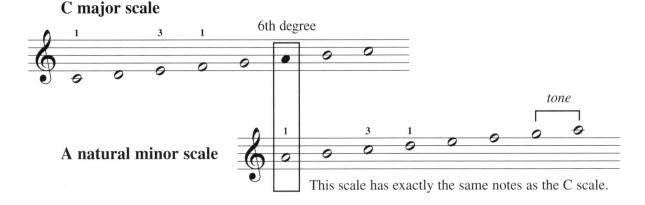

C major scale

6th degree

A natural minor scale

tone

This scale has exactly the same notes as the C scale.

A Natural Minor Scale

2. Practise hands separately, then hands together.

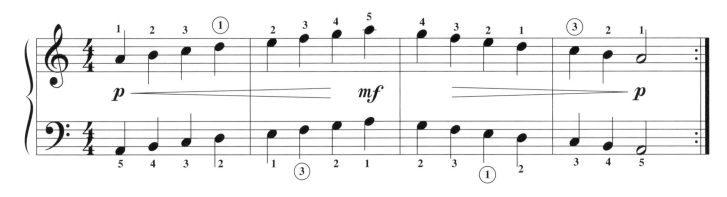

For the harmonic minor scale, raise the 7th note a semitone.
This creates a semitone between scale degrees 7 and 8—the *leading note* to the *tonic*.

A Harmonic Minor Scale

3. Practise hands separately, then hands together.

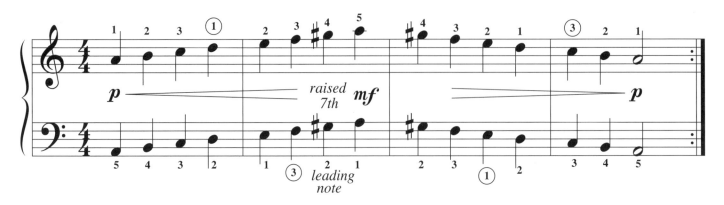

raised
7th

leading
note

Primary Chords in A Minor: i   iv   V7

4. Practise hands separately, then hands together.

In a minor key, the **i** and **iv** chords are minor and shown in **lower case Roman numerals**.

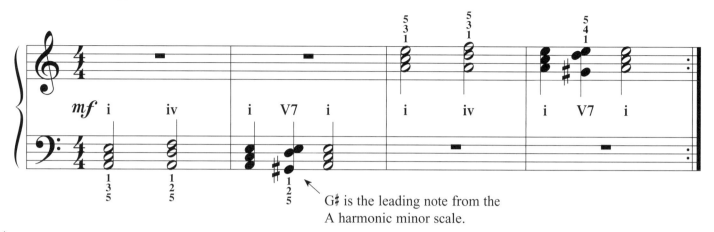

G♯ is the leading note from the A harmonic minor scale.

5. Now play this L.H. Alberti bass pattern.

Roman numerals: **i**   **iv**   **i**   **V7**   **i**

Challenge: Two-Octave A Minor Scales*

6. Practise these scales s-l-o-w-l-y.

- First play *without* the G♯ to form the **A natural minor scale**.

- Repeat *with* the G♯ to form the **A harmonic minor scale**.

*Teacher Note: The melodic minor scale is introduced in Level 4-5.

March Slav

Key of A Minor

Peter Ilyich Tchaikovsky
(1840-1893, Russia)
arranged

Slow march ($\quad$ = 72)

Leger Lines

Leger lines are short lines used to extend the stave.

Reading Hint

Remember the letter names **A-C-E** on the **LINE NOTES**.
This pattern can help you learn UPPER, INNER, and LOWER leger notes.

- Play, noticing the A-C-E pattern.

Upper Leger Notes

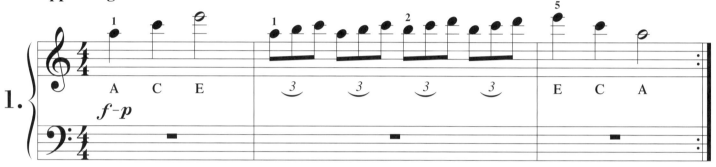

Inner Leger Notes

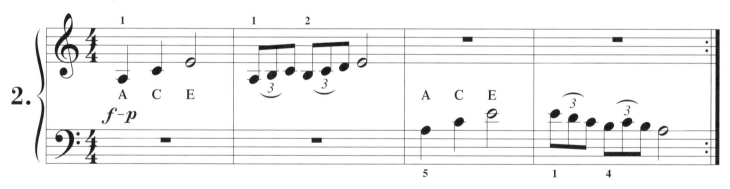

Lower Leger Notes

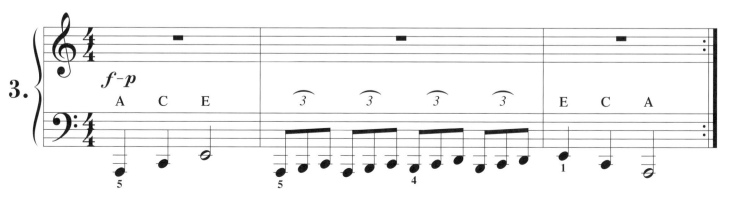

Tech & Perf page 20 (Ski Trail) 33

sfz – *sforzando*

A sudden, strong accent
on a single note or chord.

Fiesta España

Key of _____ Major/Minor (circle)

Allegro (♩ = 160–176)

N. Faber

Tech & Perf page 21 (The Windy Chase)

DISCOVERY

Name the four **chords** used in this piece: ___ minor ___ major ___ major ___ major

Playing a Lead Sheet

A *lead sheet* consists of a melody with **chord symbols** shown above the stave.
The chord symbols indicate the harmony to be played with your left hand.

Directions for Greensleeves:

- First, play the melody alone (page 37).

- Next, play the Solid Chord Warm-up below.

- Now play the melody with **solid chords** on
  beat 1 of each bar. Follow the chord symbols.

Solid Chord Warm-up

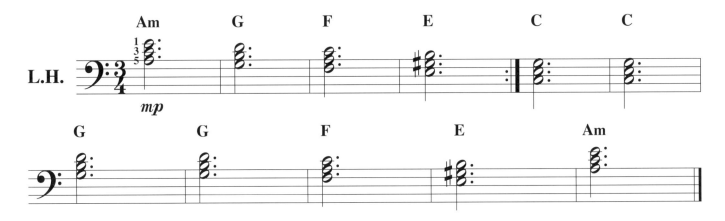

- Now practise this Broken Chord Warm-up.

- Challenge: Play the melody slowly with this
  L.H. accompaniment. See the example below.

Broken Chord Warm-up

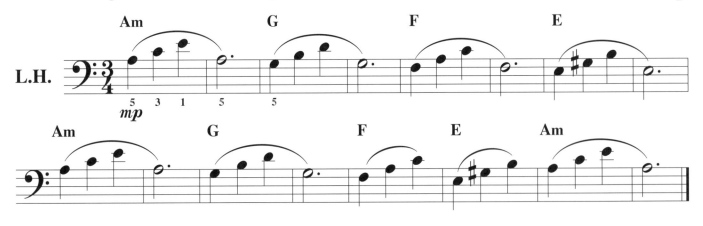

Example:

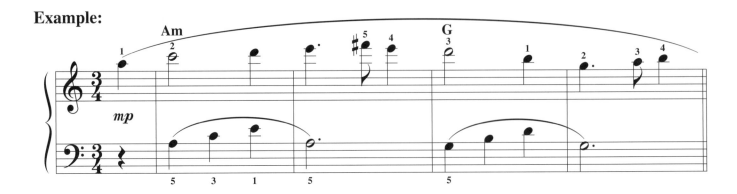

Lead Sheet for
Greensleeves

Key of ____ Major/Minor

Flowing smoothly (♩ = 108-120)

English Folk Song
arranged

Chord symbols: Am   G

cross over

A - las, my love,____ you do me wrong____ to

5   F   E   Am

cast me off____ dis - cour - teous - ly. And I have

10   G   F   E

loved____ you oh so long,____ de - light - ing in____ your

15 Am   C   G

com - pa - ny. Green - sleeves____ was all my joy.

21 F   E   C

Green - sleeves____ was my de - light. Green - sleeves was my

27 G   F   E   Am

heart of gold,____ and who but my la - dy Green - sleeves.

DISCOVERY

Play using the pedal. Hint: Pedal for each chord change.

Write A Minor Scales: Natural and Harmonic

1. Write the **A NATURAL minor scale** for each clef. Then write the fingering in the blanks.

fingering: __1__ ___ ___ ___ ___ ___ ___ ___

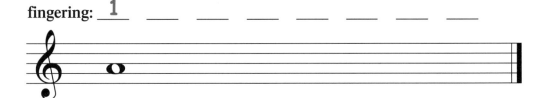

natural

fingering: __5__ ___ ___ ___ ___ ___ ___ ___

2. For the **HARMONIC minor scale**, the 7th degree is raised a _____ to form the *leading note*.

3. • Now write the **A HARMONIC minor scale** in each clef. Include the ♯ for the raised 7th.
  • Write **T** below the tonic, **D** below the dominant, and **LN** below the leading note.

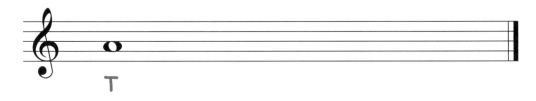

harmonic

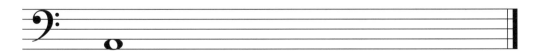

4. Copy the example below to practise finding the **relative minor key** from C major. Remember, the keys of C major and A minor share the *same* key signature.

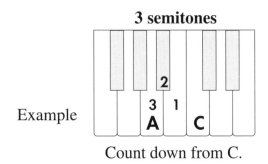

Example

Count down from C.

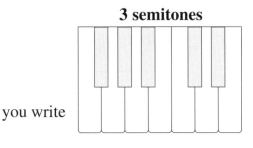

you write

5. Close your eyes and *listen*. Your teacher will play an **A NATURAL minor** or an **A HARMONIC minor** scale in various octaves. Identify the scale that was played.

EAR TRAINING

Harmonise in A Minor: i, iv, and V7 Chords

1. Copy each chord and its Roman numeral.
Notice the **i** and **iv** chords are **minor** and use lower case Roman numerals.

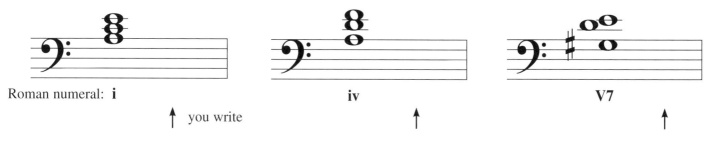

Roman numeral: **i**   **iv**   **V7**

↑ you write

2. • First play the R.H. melody.

• Then harmonise it with **i**, **iv**, or **V7** chords.
Play with solid chords.

Fiesta Dance

3. • Name both **leger line notes** and the **interval** formed in each example.

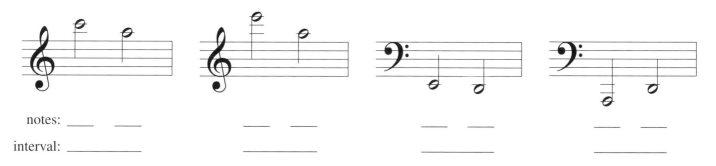

notes: _____   _____   _____   _____

interval: _____   _____   _____   _____

Key of D Minor

The key of D minor is the RELATIVE MINOR of F major.

D minor and **F major** share the same key signature: 1 flat.

Review: Think 3 semitones down from the tonic of the major key.

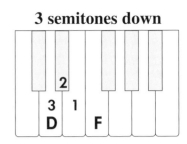

3 semitones down

1. Play each scale and *listen* to the sound.

F major scale

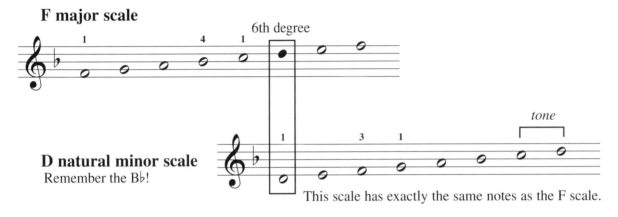

D natural minor scale
Remember the B♭!

This scale has exactly the same notes as the F scale.

2. Practise hands separately, then hands together.

D Natural Minor Scale

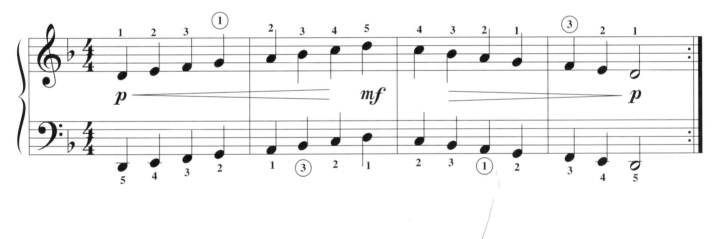

Remember, for the harmonic minor scale, raise the 7th note a semitone.
This creates a semitone between scale degrees 7 and 8—the *leading note* to the *tonic*.

D Harmonic Minor Scale

3. Practise hands separately, then hands together.

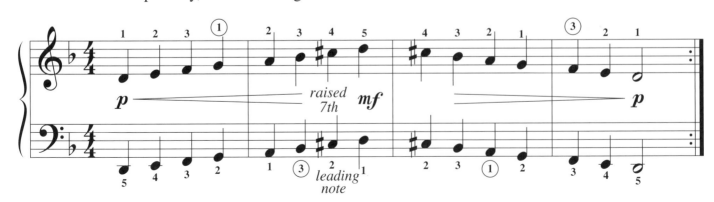

Primary Chords in D Minor: i   iv   V7

4. Practise hands separately, then hands together.
In a minor key, the **i** and **iv** chords are minor.

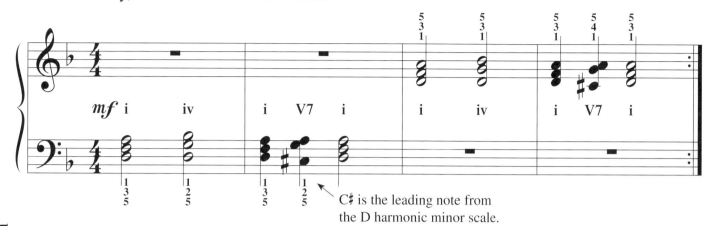

C♯ is the leading note from
the D harmonic minor scale.

5. Now play this L.H. Alberti bass pattern.

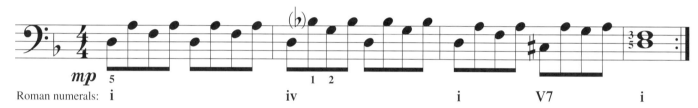

Roman numerals: i   iv   i   V7   i

Challenge: Two-Octave D Minor Scales

6. Practise these scales s-l-o-w-l-y.

- First play *without* the C♯ to form the **D natural minor scale**.

- Repeat *with* the C♯ to form the **D harmonic minor scale**.

The *character* of a piece refers to the mood of the music.
This piece has two different sections, each with its own character and tempo.

Tempo I—Slowly, with drama, in $\frac{4}{4}$
Tempo II—Quickly, mischievously, in ¢

• Create the contrasting moods of this piece
  with your fine technique and artistry!

Gypsy Camp

Key of _____ Major/Minor

N. Faber

🎵 Tech & Perf pages 24-25 (Racecar Scales), pages 26-27 (Magic Carpet Variations)

molto means "very." Make a big ritardando for *molto rit.*

D.C. al Fine

Harmony Check: Name the harmony for *bars 1-8* as **i**, **iv**, or **V7**.

Review: Swing Rhythm (See page 12)
Play the quavers in a *long-short* pattern.

- First play hands together with **even quavers**.

- Then play the quavers in a *long-short* swing pattern!

Lonesome Sailor Blues*

Key of ____ Major/Minor

Traditional

*originally titled *The St. James Infirmary*

44   Tech & Perf page 28 (Shepherd Pipes), page 29 (Minuet in D Minor)

swing the quavers!

Write D Minor Scales: Natural and Harmonic

1. • Write the **D minor key signature**, then the **D NATURAL minor scale** for each clef.
   • Shade the *flattened* notes. Write the fingering in the blanks.

natural

2. • Write the **D minor key signature**, then the **D HARMONIC minor scale** for each clef.
   Shade the *flattened* notes. Be sure to include the ♯ for the raised 7th.
   • Write **T** below the tonic, **D** below the dominant, and **LN** below the leading note.

harmonic

3. Copy the example below to practise finding the relative minor key from F major.

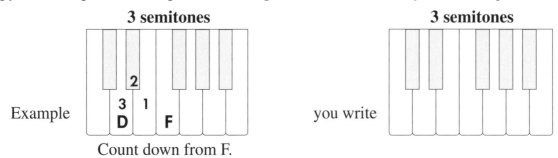

4. Close your eyes. Your teacher will play a **major** scale, **natural minor** scale, or **harmonic minor** scale. Listen and identify the scale that was played.

Harmonise in D Minor: i, iv, and V7 Chords

1. Copy each chord and its Roman numeral.
Remember, the **i** and **iv** chords are **minor** and use lower case Roman numerals.

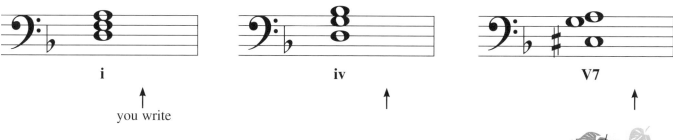

i   iv   V7

↑   ↑   ↑

you write

2. • Label the harmony for each bar as **i**, **iv**, or **V7**.

• Then compose a melody using the **D harmonic minor scale** and write it on the stave. The optional rhythm may help you.

Compose an Autumn Waltz

Waltz bass

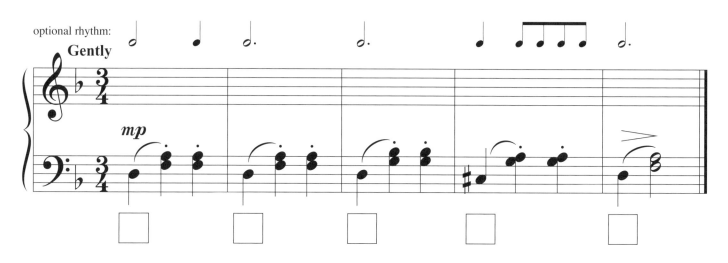

Alberti bass

Compose a Classical March

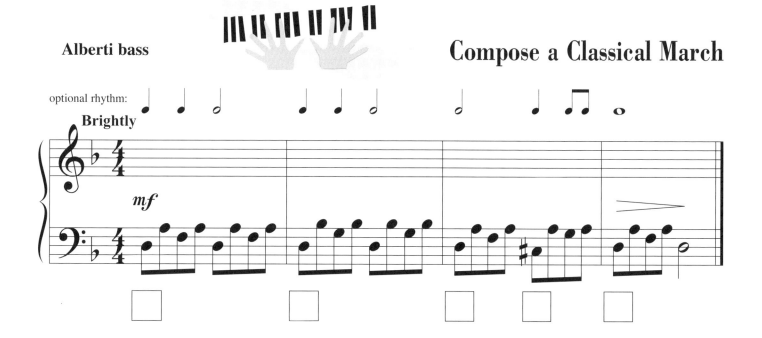

New Time Signature

$\frac{3}{8}$ = **3 beats** in a bar.

the **quaver** (♪) gets 1 beat.

In $\frac{3}{8}$ time:

quaver ♪ = 1 beat   quaver rest ♪ = 1 beat

crotchet ♩ = 2 beats   crotchet rest 𝄽 = 2 beats

dotted crotchet ♩. = 3 beats   semibreve rest ▬ = 3 beats

 **Rhythm Patterns**

• Tap and count these $\frac{3}{8}$ rhythms with your teacher:

a.
1 2 3 | 1 2 3 | 1 2 3 | 1 2 3

b.
1 2 3 | 1 2 3 | 1 2 3 | 1 2 3

c.
1 2 3 | 1 2 3 | 1 2 3 | 1 2 3

d.
1 2 3 | 1 2 3 | 1 2 3 | 1 2 3

• Can you tap **rhythm a** while your teacher taps **rhythm b**? Try different combinations!

New Time Signature

$\dfrac{6}{8}$ =
6 beats in a bar.

the **quaver** (♪) gets one beat.

Think of $\dfrac{6}{8}$ as a combination of $\dfrac{3}{8}$ + $\dfrac{3}{8}$: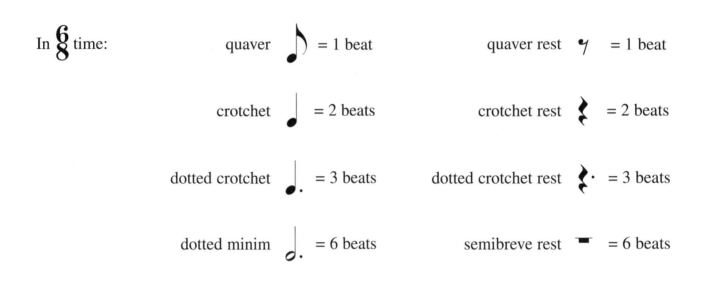

In $\dfrac{6}{8}$ time:

quaver	♪ = 1 beat		quaver rest ♭ = 1 beat	
crotchet	♩ = 2 beats		crotchet rest 𝄽 = 2 beats	
dotted crotchet	♩. = 3 beats		dotted crotchet rest 𝄽· = 3 beats	
dotted minim	♩. = 6 beats		semibreve rest ▬ = 6 beats	

- Circle each group of three beats—two circles per bar.

- Tap and count these $\dfrac{6}{8}$ rhythms with your teacher:

Rhythm Patterns

a.
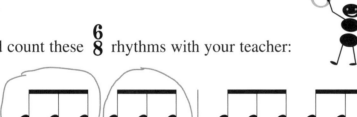

b.

c.

- Can you tap **rhythm a** while your teacher taps **rhythm b**? Try different combinations!

Sleigh Ride Holiday

Traditional melody

Campbells Are Coming

Key of _____ Major/Minor

• First, draw bar lines from *bars 13-24*.

Traditional, Scotland
arranged

With spirit (♩. = 96-108)

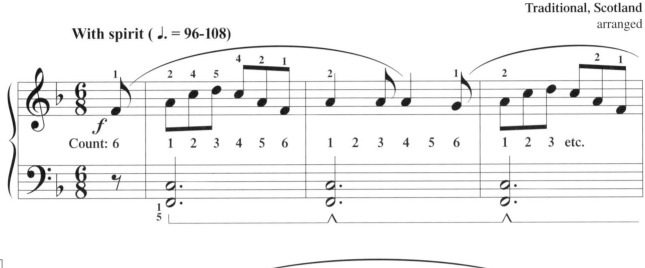

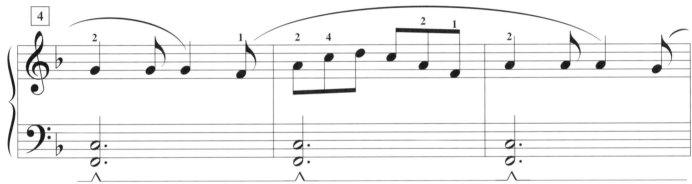

Tech & Perf pages 34-35 (Aurora Borealis)

DISCOVERY

Can you transpose *bars 1-8* to the key of **C major**? To **G major**?

⁶⁄₈ at a Fast Tempo

In fast tempos, ⁶⁄₈ is felt with **2 beats** per bar.
The ♩. gets the beat.

• Tap this rhythm, counting aloud:

⁶⁄₈ ♩. ♩. | ♪♪♪ ♩. ‖
   1   2   1 + a 2

Funiculì, Funiculà*

Key of _____ Major/Minor

Luigi Denza
(1846-1922, Italy)
arranged

Moderato, "in two" (♩. = 104-120)

mf
Some think_____ the world is
think_____ it well is to

made for fun and frol - ic,_____ and so do
be all mel - an - chol - ic,_____ to pine and

I! And so do I!
sigh, but no, not I!

1. Some
2. Hark - en! Hark - en!
f

DISCOVERY

Harmony Check: Find seven consecutive bars of the **V7** chord.

*This Italian song was written to celebrate the opening of a *funicular railway* (a mountain cable car) that went to the top of Mt. Vesuvius.

Rhythm Talk in $\frac{3}{8}$

1. $\frac{3}{8}$ = ___ beats in a bar *(fill in)*

   the _____ gets one beat

2. Copy these patterns. Write the counts under the correct beats.

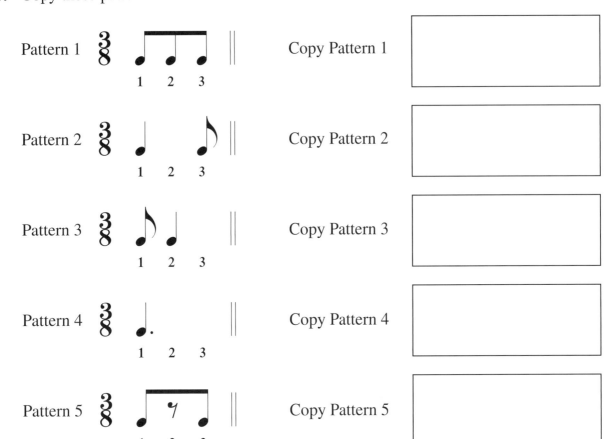

Pattern 1   Copy Pattern 1

Pattern 2   Copy Pattern 2

Pattern 3   Copy Pattern 3

Pattern 4   Copy Pattern 4

Pattern 5   Copy Pattern 5

3. Write the counts under these melodies. Then play, counting aloud.

4. Write four bars of your own rhythm. Think patterns! See Patterns 1-5 above.
   Then tap your rhythm.

   (you write)

Rhythm Talk in 6/8

1. 6/8 = ___ beats in a bar *(fill in)*

the _____ gets one beat

2. Copy these patterns. Write the counts under the correct beats.

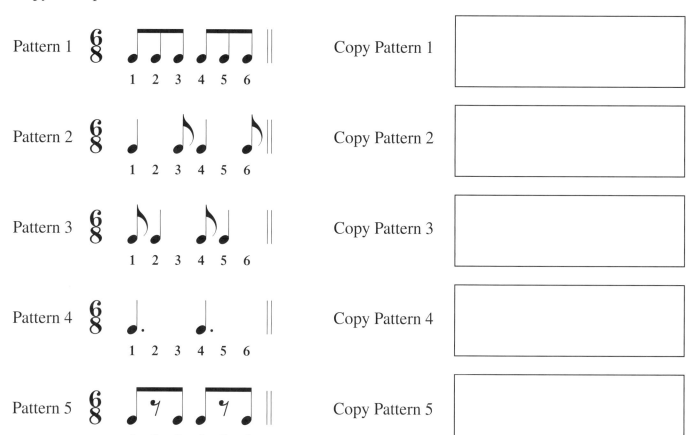

Pattern 1 — Copy Pattern 1

Pattern 2 — Copy Pattern 2

Pattern 3 — Copy Pattern 3

Pattern 4 — Copy Pattern 4

Pattern 5 — Copy Pattern 5

3. Write the correct time signature for each example: 2/4 3/4 4/4 3/8 6/8

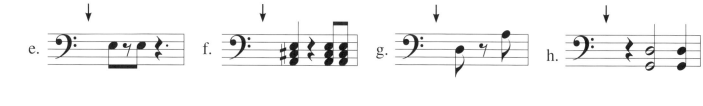

4. Write four bars of your own rhythms. Think 3/8 + 3/8. Then tap your rhythm.

(you write)

The D Major Scale

Remember, a major scale has 7 notes called **scale degrees**.

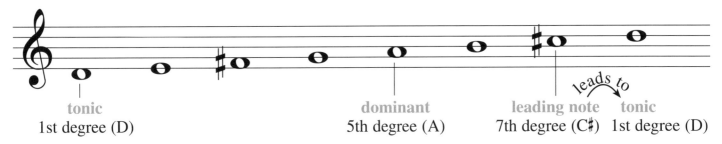

tonic
1st degree (D)

dominant
5th degree (A)

leads to

leading note
7th degree (C♯)

tonic
1st degree (D)

• Play the tonic, dominant, and leading note in the key of D.

Key Signature for D Major

F♯ and C♯

• The D major scale has an F♯ and a C♯.

• A piece in the key of D major will also use F♯ and C♯.

• A sharp is not written before these notes. Instead, F♯ and C♯ are shown at the beginning of each stave. This is the **key signature** for D major.

Playing the D Major Scale

1. Practise hands separately, then hands together.

The fingering for the D major scale is the same as for the C and G major scales.

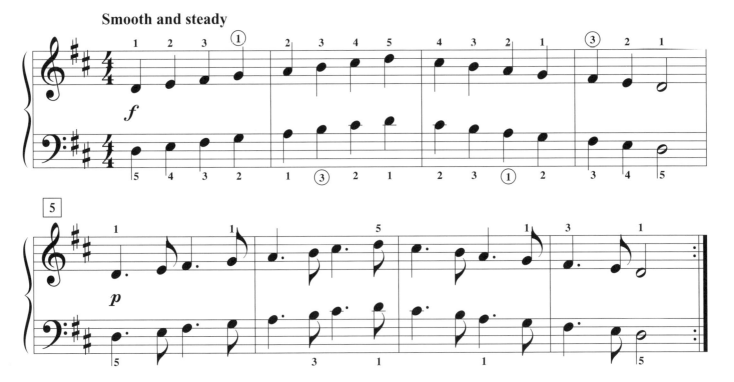

Primary Chords in D Major: I IV V7

2. Practise these primary chords. Say the Roman numerals aloud.

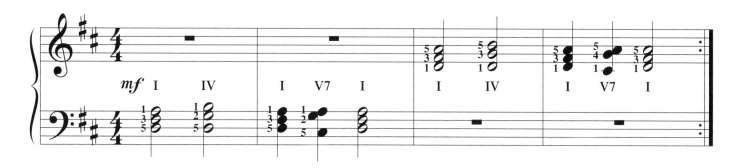

3. Now play this L.H. Alberti bass pattern.

Challenge: Two-Octave D Major Scales

4. • Practise these **D major** scales.

• Then play two-octave scales in **C major** and **G major**. The fingering is the same.

Musical Form: Binary or AB

Binary form or **AB** form means two sections—
an **A** section followed by a **B** section.

Allegro in D Major

James Hook
(1746-1827, England)
original form
(transposed from C major)

- Write **A** or **B** in the boxes given.

*Optional: Your teacher will show you how to
add this special ornamentation called a **mordent**.

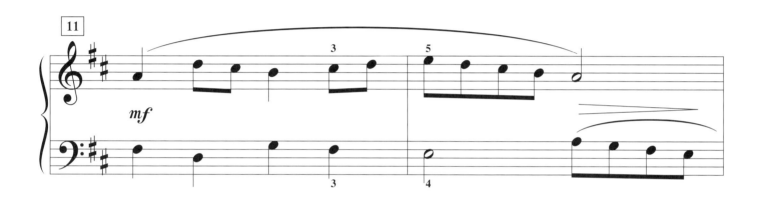

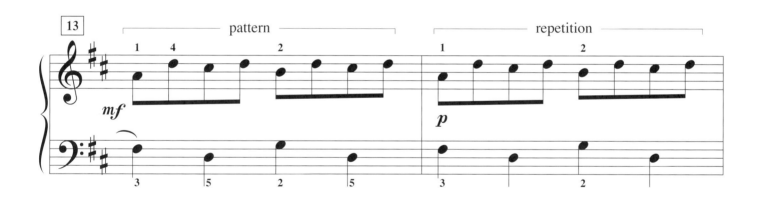

DISCOVERY

Can you transpose this piece to **C major**?

Tchaikovsky's Theme
from *Piano Concerto No. 1*, 2nd Movement

Key of _____ Major

- Feel the "big beats" on counts 1 and 4.
  This will help the music flow.

Peter Ilyich Tchaikovsky
(1840-1893, Russia)
arranged

Tech & Perf pages 40-43 (Song of Kilimanjaro)

DISCOVERY

Harmony Check: Which line of music uses only the **D major** chord?

Write the D Major Scale

1. Fill in the blanks.

The D major scale has 7 notes created from _____ and _____.

The **semitones** occur between degrees ____ and ____ and degrees ____ and ____ .

All the other intervals are _____.

2. Trace, then copy the **D major key signature** three times. Name the two sharps.

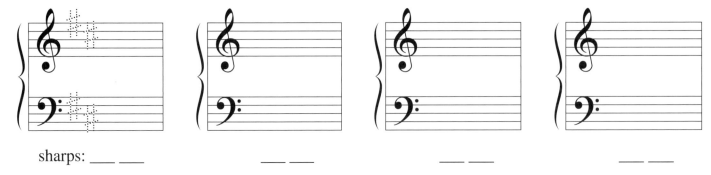

sharps: ___ ___   ___ ___   ___ ___   ___ ___

3. • Write the D major scale for each clef. Draw **sharps** in front of the correct notes.
   • Number the scale degrees 1–8.
   • Use a ⌐⌐ to mark the *tones*. Use a ∨ to mark the *semitones*.

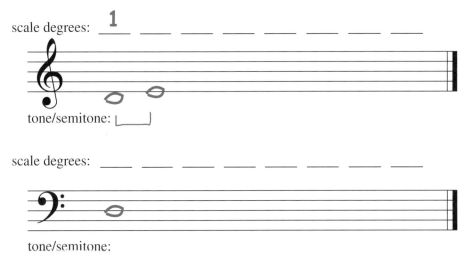

"Canoe Ride" Improvisation

4. *Listen* to the teacher accompaniment. When ready, improvise a melody using notes from the D major scale **in any order**. Remember the **F♯** and **C♯**!

• Play D major solid and broken chords.

• Play repeated notes, especially on the *tonic* (D) and *dominant* (A).

• Make up short musical patterns. Repeat them *forte* and then *piano*.

Teacher Duet: (Student improvises higher using the D major scale.)

Harmonise in D Major: I, IV, and V7 Chords

1. Copy each chord and its Roman numeral.

I

↑ you write

IV

↑

V7

↑

2.
- First play the R.H. melody.
- Then harmonise it with **I**, **IV**, or **V7** chords.
  Play with solid chords.

Street Dance

Ex. I

3. Can you transpose the melody and chords for *Street Dance* DOWN a tone to **C major**?

Leger Line Review

4. Name the intervals formed by these leger line notes.

interval: _____   _____   _____

_____   _____   _____

The Chromatic Scale

A chromatic scale has **12** notes, each a **semitone** apart. Every black and white key is played.

1. Play a R.H. chromatic scale up and down. Look at the keyboard diagram, then the music.

- Use finger 3 for every black key.

- Use finger 1 for every white key except the white-key semitones E-F and B-C.

Repeat on HIGHER Es.

2. Play a L.H. chromatic scale down and up. Look at the keyboard diagram, then the music.

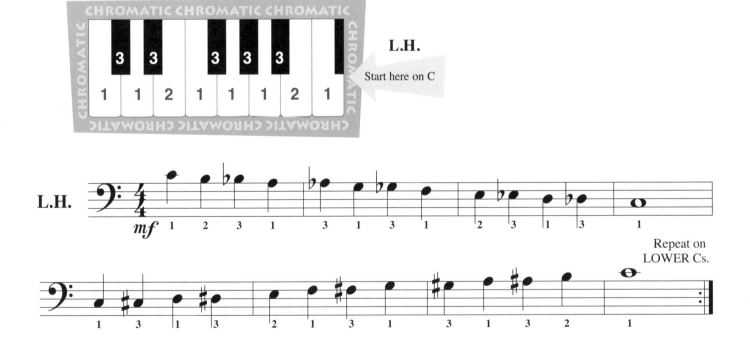

Repeat on LOWER Cs.

Super Scale Challenge:

- Starting on Middle E, play a R.H. chromatic scale up to the top of the keyboard and back down again.

- Starting on Middle C, play a L.H. chromatic scale down to the bottom of the keyboard and back up again.

This piece is built on the chromatic scale.

- Use a closed, cupped hand position for the chromatic passages.

- Notice the tempo mark. Play the quavers in a *long-short* swing pattern!

Alley Cat Swing

Key of _____ Major/Minor

N. Faber

Moderate swing (♩ = 120-132)

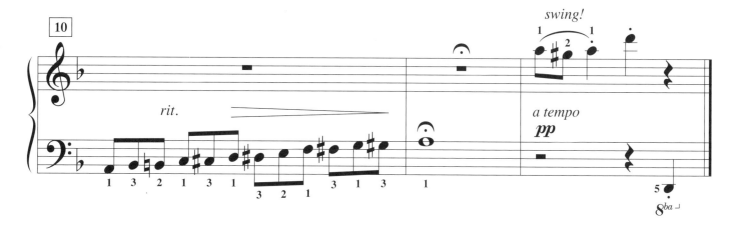

Acciaccatura

A small note with a slash. It is an ornamental note, played quickly into the note that follows.

- Practise these examples. Your teacher will help.

Phantom of the Keys

Key of ____ Major/Minor

Mischievous, with energy (♩=88-100)

N. Faber

🐦 Tech & Perf pages 46-47 (The Fly's Adventure)

DISCOVERY Is the G♯ sharp in *bar 9* from the **natural minor** or **harmonic minor** scale?
Is G♯ the tonic, dominant, or leading note in the key of A minor?

Write the Chromatic Scale

1. • Name the notes of the *ascending* chromatic scale. Notice as the scale goes up, **sharps** are used.

note names: ___ ___ ___ ___ ___ ___ ___ ___ ___ ___ ___ ___ ___

• Copy the ascending chromatic scale above. Remember to use sharps!
• Write the R.H. fingering in the blanks below. You may check yourself at the piano.

fingering: ___ ___ ___ ___ ___ ___ ___ ___ ___ ___ ___ ___ ___

2. • Name the notes of the *descending* chromatic scale. Notice as the scale goes down, **flats** are used.

note names: ___ ___ ___ ___ ___ ___ ___ ___ ___ ___ ___ ___ ___

• Copy the descending chromatic scale above. Remember to use flats!
• Write the L.H. fingering in the blanks below. You may check yourself at the piano.

fingering: ___ ___ ___ ___ ___ ___ ___ ___ ___ ___ ___ ___ ___

3. Circle 3 examples that use the chromatic scale. Think *semitones!*

4. Your teacher will play a **major** scale, a **minor** scale, or a **chromatic** scale. *Listen* and circle the one you hear.

Teacher Note: Create your own examples.

UNIT 9

One-Octave Arpeggios

To play a one-handed *arpeggio*, the hand is extended over the keys.

- For the right hand, use a circular **"under and over"** motion of the wrist.
  Notice the fingering is **1-2-3-5**.

- Continue this white-key pattern with **Em**, **F**, **G**, and **Am** chords.

- For the left hand, use a circular **"over and under"** motion of the wrist.
  Notice the fingering is **5-4-2-1**.

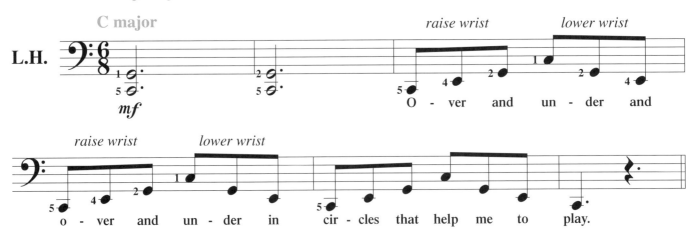

- Continue this white-key pattern with **Dm**, **Em**, **F**, **G**, and **Am** chords.

72

The accompaniment in this piece is based on one-octave arpeggios.

- First practise the L.H. separately. Use the crotchet rest to prepare the next arpeggio.

Novela*

Key of _____ Major/Minor

N. Faber

Andante (♩ = 80-92)

mp -*pp* *for entire repeat*

Novela is the Spanish word for a little story.

poco is the Italian word for little.
poco rit. means to slow down a little.

Willow Tree Waltz

Key of _____ Major

N. Faber

Tech & Perf page 49 (Fanfare Minuet)

Name One-Octave Arpeggios

- Write the **letter name** of each arpeggio and indicate *major* or *minor*.

- Write the chord notes in the blanks.

- Play each arpeggio on the piano.

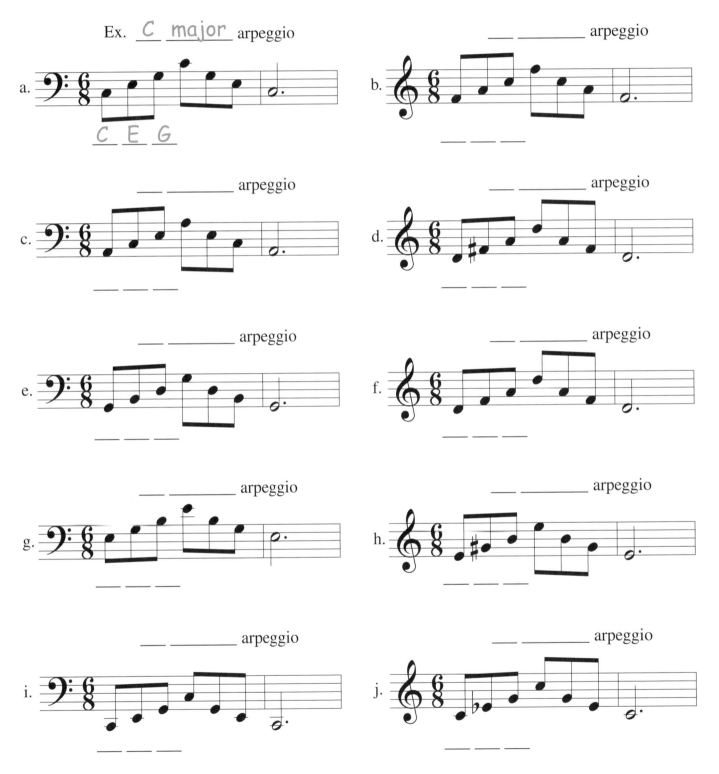

Ex. _C_ _major_ arpeggio

a. _C_ _E_ _G_

b. ___ _____ arpeggio

c. ___ _____ arpeggio

d. ___ _____ arpeggio

e. ___ _____ arpeggio

f. ___ _____ arpeggio

g. ___ _____ arpeggio

h. ___ _____ arpeggio

i. ___ _____ arpeggio

j. ___ _____ arpeggio

Close your eyes and *listen!* Your teacher will play a **major** or **minor** one-octave arpeggio. Say "major" or "minor" for what you hear.

Teacher Note: Choose various major or minor one-octave arpeggios to play.

The 12 Major and Minor Triads

A triad is a 3-note chord built in 3rds.
The 3 notes of a triad are the **root**, **3rd**, and **5th**.

5th
3rd
root

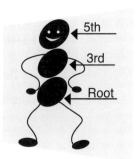

- Practise this triad exercise going up the keyboard **chromatically** (by semitones).

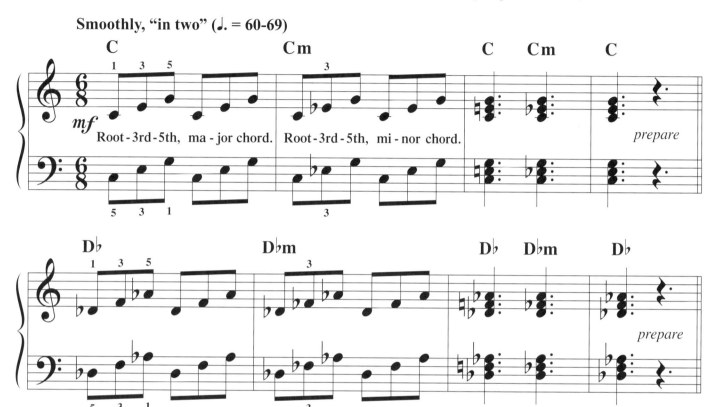

- Use the chart below to continue, beginning on **D**, **E♭**, **E**, **F**, **F♯**, **G**, **A♭**, **A**, **B♭**, **B**, and **C**.

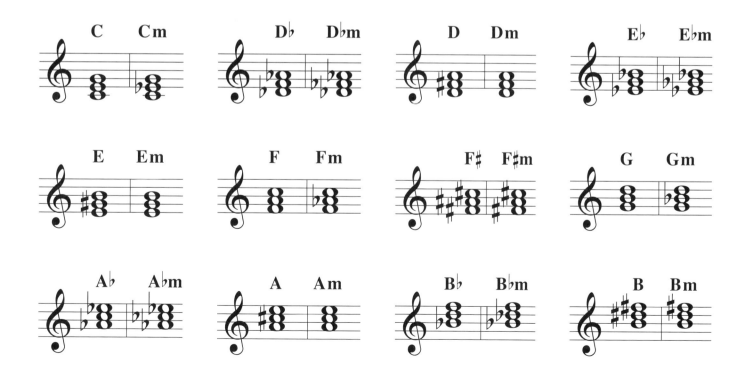

New Time Signature

$\frac{6}{4}$ = 6 beats in a bar
the ♩ gets the beat

Think of $\frac{6}{4}$ as a combination of $\frac{3}{4} + \frac{3}{4}$:

♩ ♩ ♩ + ♩ ♩ ♩

Liebestraum

(Dream of Love, No. 3)

Key of _____ Major/Minor

Franz Liszt
(1811–1886, Hungary)
arranged

Allegro moderato (♩ = 104-120)

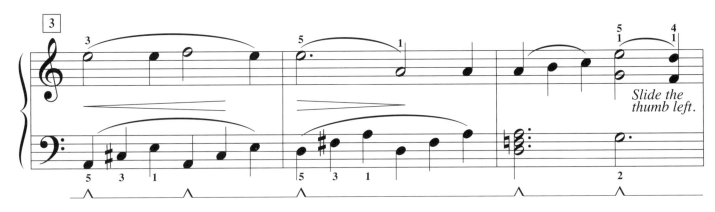

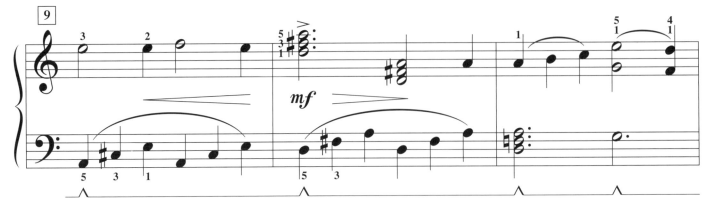

Arpeggiated or Rolled Chord: The wavy line indicates to play the notes quickly, bottom to top.

Chord Inversions: Three Positions for Triads

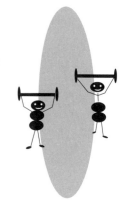

The notes of a triad can be rearranged, or *inverted*. The letter names stay the same.
Every triad has 3 positions: **root position**, **1st inversion**, and **2nd inversion**.

• Play these 3 positions for the C major triad. *Listen* to the sound!

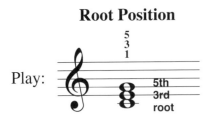
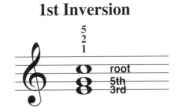
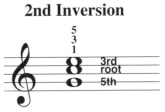

The **root** is the lowest note.   The **3rd** is the lowest note.   The **5th** is the lowest note.

The chord name (root) is the *upper note* of the interval of a **4th**.

• Watch as your teacher demonstrates.

• Your turn! Play slowly and memorise.

1. C Major Chord Inversions

2. G Major Chord Inversions

- Transpose to **A minor**, **D minor**, and **F major**.

- Write the **chord letter names** in the boxes. Remember the chord root is the *upper note* of the 4th.

Inversion Etude

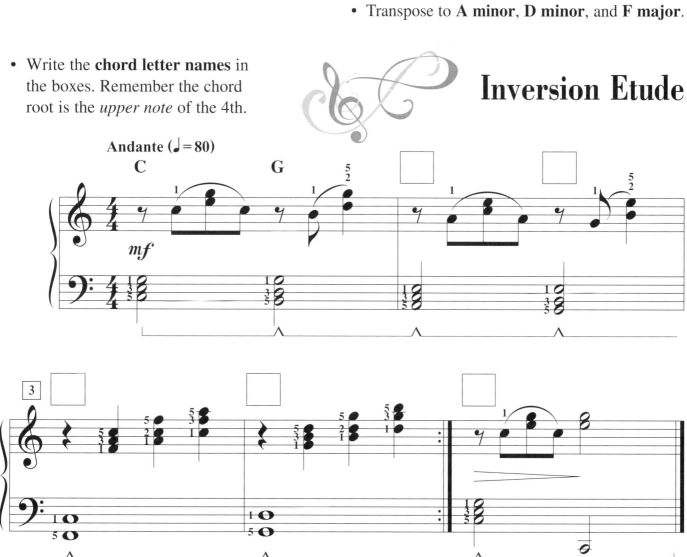

A gavotte is a dance in moderate $\frac{4}{4}$ time, popularized in 18th century France.

Rounded Binary Form

When part of the A section returns *within* the B section, the form is **rounded binary**.

Gavotte

Benjamin Carr
(1768-1831, U.S.A.)
original form

Moderato (♩ = 108-120)

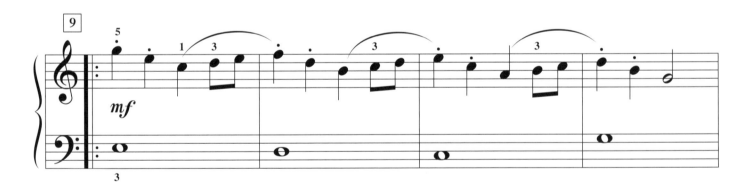

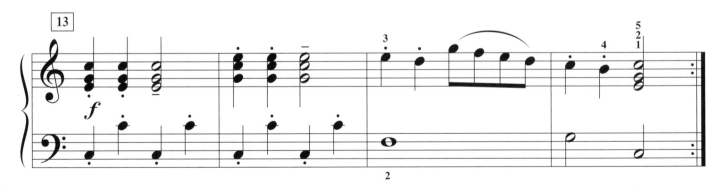

DISCOVERY

Can you memorise *Gavotte?*

- First play slowly feeling **6 beats** per bar.

- When ready, play *vivace* feeling **2 beats** per bar.

The Return

Cornelius Gurlitt
(1820-1901, Germany)
original form

loco – as written
This word occurs after an 8va sign.
(See *bar 26.*)

Ceremony for Peace

Key of _____ Major

N. Faber

Tech & Perf pages 52-53 (Emperor's Legend)

Chord Inversion Quiz

1. Review:

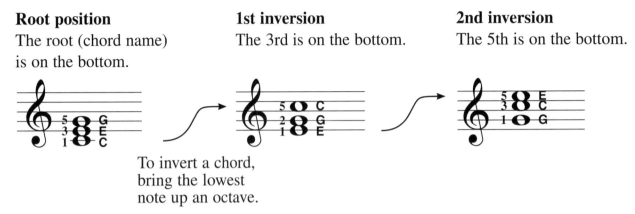

Root position
The root (chord name) is on the bottom.

1st inversion
The 3rd is on the bottom.

2nd inversion
The 5th is on the bottom.

To invert a chord, bring the lowest note up an octave.

2. • Write the following chords in **root position**, **1st inversion**, and **2nd inversion**.

   • Shade the *root* for each chord. Hint: The root is always the *upper* note of the 4th.

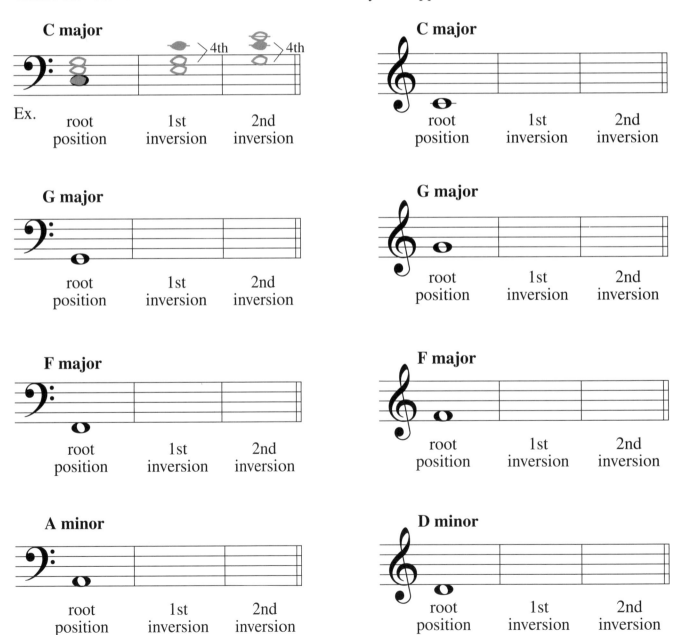

Inversion Chord Chart

3. • Study the top row. Then complete this chart for each keyboard diagram.

CHORD	chord root	position	major/minor	on the stave
Ex. [keyboard: E G C]	*C*	root pos. (1st inv.) 2nd inv.	(major) minor	[treble clef chord]
[keyboard: D F A]		root pos. 1st inv. 2nd inv.	major minor	[bass clef]
[keyboard: E A C]		root pos. 1st inv. 2nd inv.	major minor	[treble clef]
[keyboard: G C E]		root pos. 1st inv. 2nd inv.	major minor	[bass clef]
[keyboard: F A D]		root pos. 1st inv. 2nd inv.	major minor	[treble clef]
[keyboard: F A C]		root pos. 1st inv. 2nd inv.	major minor	[bass clef]
[keyboard: F# A D]		root pos. 1st inv. 2nd inv.	major minor	[treble clef]

4. Close your eyes and *listen* to the chord pattern your teacher plays. It will begin in root position but end in **root position**, **1st**, or **2nd inversion**. Name the last chord you hear.

Teacher Note: Create your own chord inversion patterns. Three examples are given below.

87

Semiquavers
(16th Notes)

Four semiquavers = one crotchet

Drummer at the Keyboard

- On the closed keyboard lid, tap your R.H. and L.H. together as you count aloud. Can you tap with the metronome at ♩ = **69**?

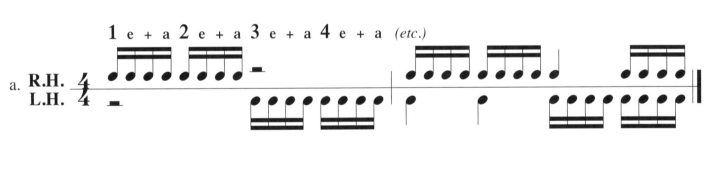

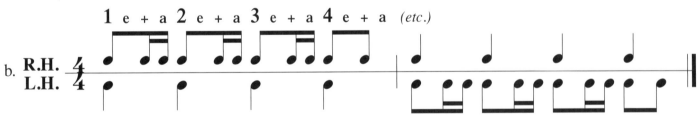

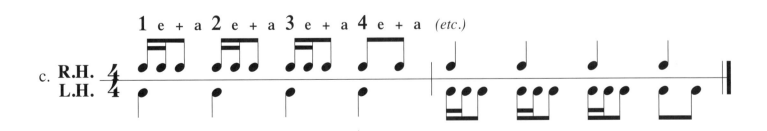

Write Semiquaver Rhythms

1. Fill up each box by writing rhythm patterns that use **semiquavers**.
Include patterns like these:

2. Can you tap the rhythms you created on the closed keyboard lid?

3. Your teacher will choose a key on the piano and play either **example a** or **example b**.
Listen carefully and circle the one you hear.

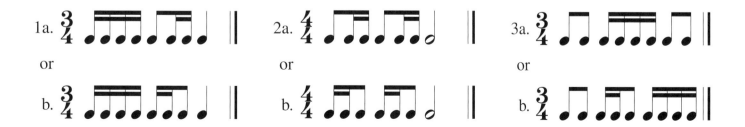

Extra Credit: Do this ear-training activity with your teacher as the student.
You tap either **example a** or **example b** on the closed keyboard cover.
Did your teacher select the correct rhythm? Have fun!

Rage Over a Lost Penny

adapted from Op. 129*

Key of _____ Major

Hint: First practise the R.H. separately.
Notice the fingering.

Ludwig van Beethoven
(1770-1827, Germany)
arranged

*Op. is the abbreviation for *opus* (work).

Tech & Perf page 55 (Scale Journey), page 56 (Adagio and Allegro)

This piece is in **A B A** form (also called ternary form).
Label the **A** section, **B** section, and **A** section in your music.

A Closer Look at Harmony

- Play these chords built on the C scale.
  Notice that the I, IV, and V chords are **major**. The ii, iii, and vi chords are **minor**.

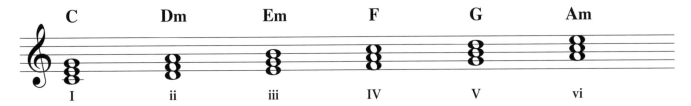

- The Pachelbel Canon is based on a repeating 4-bar chord pattern:

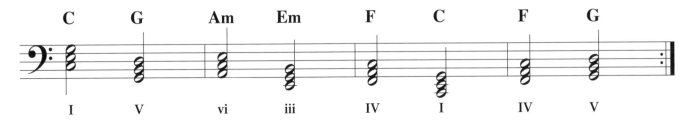

- Name the inversions used
  for the R.H. in *bars 1-4*.

Pachelbel Canon

Johann Pachelbel
(1653-1706, Germany)
arranged

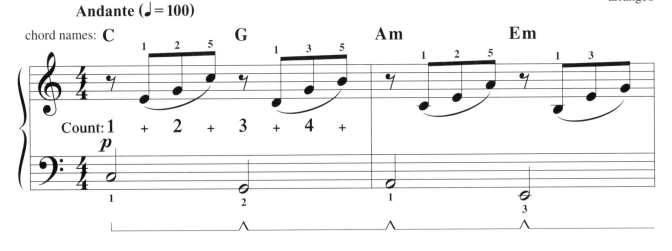

🎵 Tech & Perf pages 57-63 (Seaside Suite)

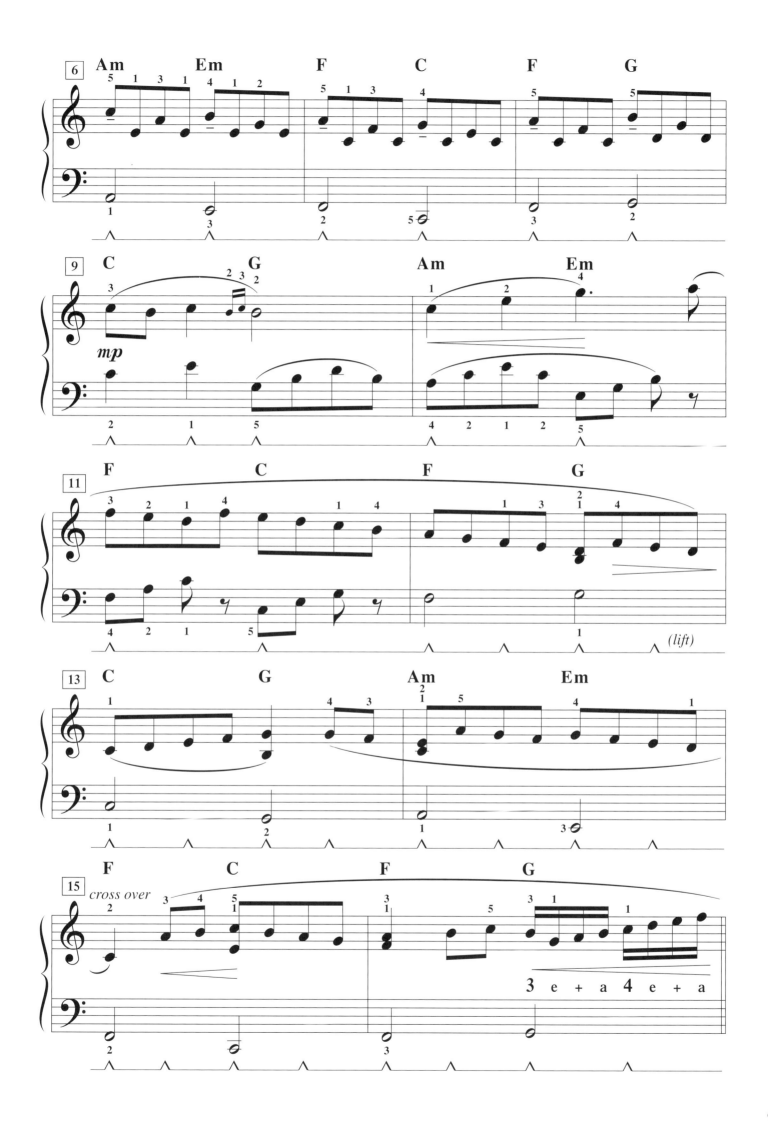

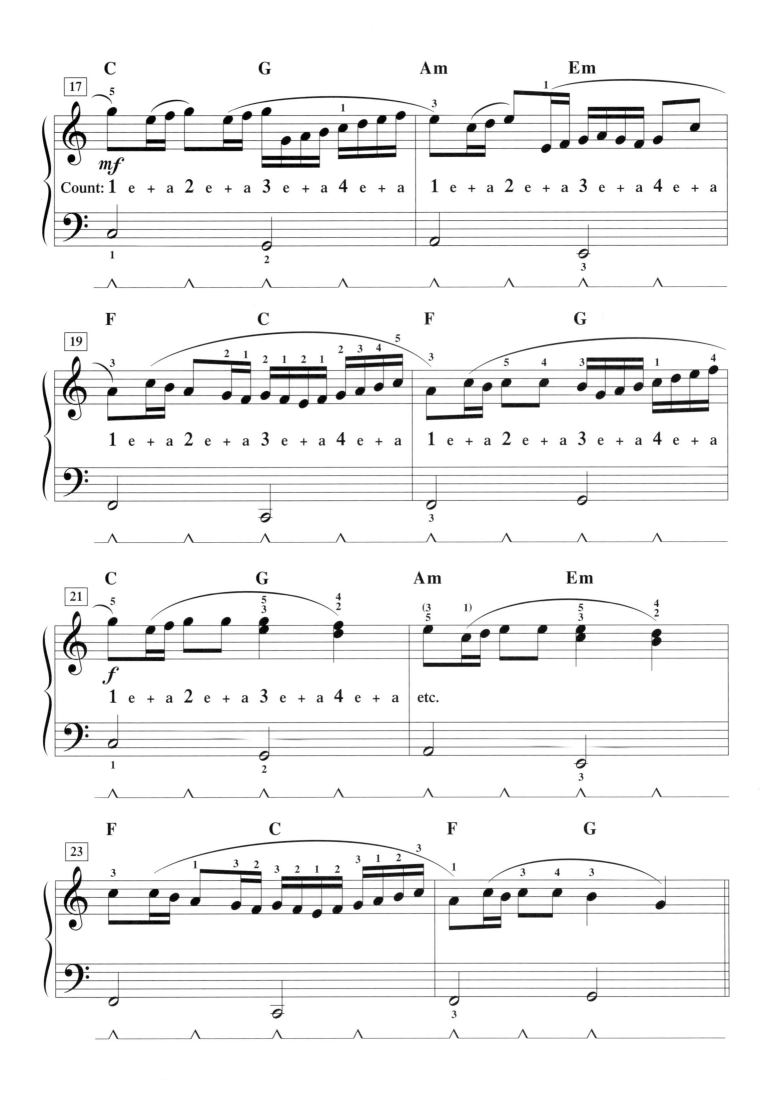

Can you play the L.H. bass line for *bars 1-4* by memory?

Certificate
of Achievement

CONGRATULATIONS TO

_____

(Your name)

You have completed

Piano Adventures® Level 3

and are now ready for

Piano Adventures® Level 4-5

Teacher: _____

Date: _____